Who's Who?

by Narinder Dhami

Illustrated by Julie Anderson

Chapter 1

Rosie, Ben, Mum and Dad were having breakfast.

"Rosie, do you want some toast?" Mum asked.

Rosie was watching TV. She didn't hear what her mum said.

"Rosie!" Mum shouted. "Do you want some toast?"

Rosie still didn't hear. So Mum turned the TV off.

"Oh, Mum!" said Rosie, "I was watching that!"

"Do you want some toast?" asked Mum.

"I hate toast!" said Rosie. "I want cheese sandwiches."

"You'll eat what I give you!" Mum said, and she gave Rosie some toast.

But Rosie didn't eat it.

"Do you want some toast, Ben?" Mum asked.

"No," said Ben, "I want chocolate ice cream."

"You can't have chocolate ice cream for breakfast!" Mum said, and she gave Ben some toast.

But Ben didn't eat it.

"Do you want some toast?" Mum asked Dad.

"I haven't got time," Dad said. "I'm already late for work."

"Eat your toast," Mum said to Rosie and Ben.

"I hate toast," Rosie said. "I want cheese sandwiches."

"And I want chocolate ice cream!" said Ben.

"Don't start, you two," said Mum. "I've got a lot of work to do today."

There was a list on the wall. It said:

"That's what I've got to do today," said Mum, "and Rosie's going to help me."

"That's not fair!" said Rosie.

"Well, I can't do all that work on my own," said Mum.

"But I wanted to sit in the garden, and read my book!" Rosie said.

"Too bad!" said Mum.

"And I've got lots of homework to do," said Rosie.

"You can do your homework later," said Mum.

Rosie was cross. "It's not fair!" she shouted. "I hate being a kid!"

"Well, it's hard work being a mum too!" said Mum.

"I don't think it's hard work at all!" said Rosie.

"Oh, don't you?" said Mum. "Well, you can be the mum today and see how you like it!"

"Cool!" said Rosie. "I'm the boss!"

Chapter 2

Ben was banging his spoon on the table.

"I want chocolate ice cream!" he shouted.

"You'd better ask Rosie," said Mum. "She's the mum today."

Rosie got the chocolate ice cream from the freezer, and gave some to Ben. He stopped shouting and started eating.

"See?" said Rosie. "It's not hard to be a mum!"

Mum smiled. She picked up her toast and her book.

"I think I'll go and eat my breakfast in the garden," she said.

Rosie made herself some cheese sandwiches. Now she was the mum, she could eat what she liked!

But then she saw what Ben had done. He had chocolate ice cream all over him!

"Look at you!" Rosie said crossly.

"You're a mess!"

Rosie had to take Ben upstairs, and get him some clean clothes to put on. Then she cleaned up the kitchen. She had to wash up, wipe the table and all the worktops, and mop the floor. It took a long time, and it was hard work.

Rosie looked out of the window. Mum was sitting in the sun, reading her book.

"It's not fair," Rosie said to herself. "Mum makes me help *her* with the housework. So now she's got to help *me*!"

Chapter 3

Rosie went into the garden.

"I want you to make the beds," she said to her mum.

"But you're the mum today!" said Mum.

"If I'm Mum, then you're Rosie," said Rosie. "So you've got to do what I say!"

Mum went upstairs and began to make the beds.

"Hurry up!" said Rosie, "I've got lots of other jobs for you to help me with!"

"I'm going as fast as I can," said Mum crossly.

"You kids are so lazy!" said Rosie.

Rosie went downstairs, and cleaned the living room. She had just finished when Ben came in. He tipped his toy-box on to the floor, and toys went everywhere.

"Ben!" Rosie shouted, "I've just cleaned up in here!"

Rosie had to clean up all over again. It was hard work, and she was tired.

Finally Rosie finished. She sat down to watch TV. Then Ben came up to her.

"What's for lunch?" he asked. "I'm starving!"

Rosie had to get up and make lunch. She made beans on toast. But Mum didn't want to eat it.

"You know I hate beans on toast, Rosie," said Mum. "Can I have pizza?"

"You'll eat what I give you!" said Rosie crossly.

Ben dropped his beans all over the floor. Rosie had to clean them up. Then she had the washing up to do.

Chapter 4

After lunch, Rosie went upstairs. She looked into her parents' bedroom. It was a mess!

"Mum!" she called. "You've got to clean up your bedroom!"

"But I want to watch TV!" said Mum. "I'll do it later."

"You'll do it now!" said Rosie. "And then I want you to get the shopping."

Mum didn't like being told what to do all the time. She cleaned up the bedroom. Then she went shopping.

It was a hot day, and Rosie had given her a very long list. Mum was tired when she got back.

Rosie looked at the shopping.

"Where's the butter?" she asked.

Mum looked at the shopping list.

"Butter isn't on the list," she said.

"I forgot it," Rosie said. "You'll have to go back to the shop and get some."

Mum went all the way back to the shop to get the butter. Rosie went on cleaning the house.

Ben came in from the garden. He had been playing in the mud.

"Look at you!" Rosie said. "You're a mess again!"

Rosie had to take Ben upstairs, and give him a bath. Then she had to clean the bathroom. Rosie was tired out. She didn't know that Mum had to work so hard.

Chapter 5

Mum came back from the shops with the butter.

"Now I'm going to watch TV," she said.

"No, now you can do your homework!" said Rosie.

"But –" said Mum.

"No buts!" said Rosie.

Mum looked at Rosie's homework. There was a lot to do. There was maths and English and history. Mum felt tired and hot. She didn't feel like doing homework at all.

Rosie started the washing, but she wasn't sure how to do it. She put all the clothes in together. All the white clothes came out pink!

When Rosie had finished the washing she sat down on the sofa. After a while, Mum sat down beside Rosie. She had done some of the homework, but she couldn't do the maths at all!

Mum and Rosie were both very tired.

"It's hard work being a mum," said Rosie.

"And it's hard work being a kid!" said Mum.

Rosie and Mum looked at each other.

"I'll help you clean the house from now on," said Rosie.

"And I won't make you eat things you don't like," said Mum.

"And I'll help you with Ben," said Rosie.

"And I won't nag you about your homework," said Mum.

Just then Dad came home from work.

"What's for dinner?" he asked.

Rosie and Mum looked at each other and smiled.

"We'll get a take-away," said Mum. "Rosie and I have worked really hard today!"